DONCASTER'S ELECTRIC TRANSPORT

Car no. 1 speeds along St Sepulchre Gate West, past butcher Poynter's shop, as it heads towards Balby.

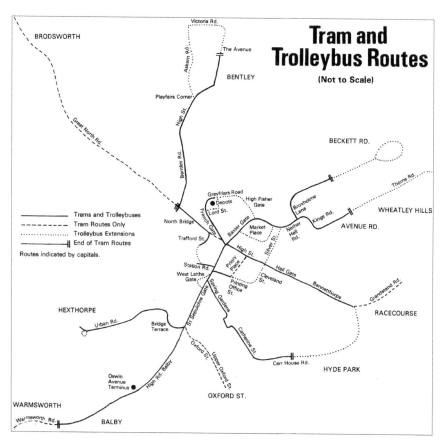

DONCASTER'S ELECTRIC TRANSPORT

PETER TUFFREY

AMBERLEY

I would like to thank the following people for their help:
Jim Firth, Hugh Parkin, Derek Porter, Alan Sutton,
Tristram Tuffrey, and Geoff Warnes.

This illustrated book is intended as a nostalgic recollection of the sixty-one years of electric transport in Doncaster, as well as a glimpse at the many interesting features and incidents of daily life along the tram and trolleybus routes. As large areas in and around Doncaster have been demolished and redeveloped since the demise of electric transport, it is hoped that the transport historian will gain added interest and that Doncaster residents will have pleasure in re-living many memories recalled by the photographs.

First published 2010

Amberley Publishing
Cirencester Road, Chalford,
Stroud, Gloucestershire, GL6 8PE

www.amberleybooks.com

Copyright © Peter Tuffrey 2010

The right of Peter Tuffrey to be identified as the
Author of this work has been asserted in accordance
with the Copyrights, Designs and Patents Act 1988.

ISBN 978-1-4456-0116-8

British Library Cataloguing in Publication Data.
A catalogue record for this book is available from
the British Library.

Typeset in 10pt on 12pt Sabon.
Typesetting and Origination by Fonthill.
Printed in the UK.

Contents

The first tram routes to Balby and Hexthorpe were opened in June 1902 at a time of great rejoicing, not only because of the dawn of a new era in street transport but because of the ending of the Boer War at that time.

Dick Kerr, car no. 24, with fifty-six seats (34/22), was bought in a batch of five vehicles, fleet nos 21-25, in 1904. It is delayed in High Street, opposite the Doncaster Mansion House, due to a point's failure. Nos 22-25 were fitted with top deck covers and direct staircases by Dick Kerr in 1913, becoming balcony cars. Nos 23 and 24 were re-trucked with seven foot six inch. Peckham P22 trucks in 1922. With the exception of no. 21 (withdrawn in 1929) all the 1904 batch of trams were withdrawn in 1930.

Karrier 'E6' D/D trolleybuses nos 357 and 365, acquired by the Doncaster Corporation in 1939, are at the YMCA adjacent to the junction of St Sepulchre Gate West and Cleveland Street. No. 365 was withdrawn in March 1956 after an accident with a lorry. No. 357 had been withdrawn earlier in December 1955.

Introduction

When trams appeared in 1902, Doncaster had undergone its first major change from a small market town into a centre of industrial importance. This was due to the establishment, by the Great Northern Railway Company, of a large engine repair works in the town in 1852-53. Around 1898, the Corporation received a proposal from the British Electrical Company Ltd to establish a tramway system between Balby and Wheatley. At a subsequent meeting, council members decided that the town should have its own electric-powered transport system.

Tram routes to Balby, Hexthorpe, Hyde Park, the Racecourse and Bentley opened in 1902. The Beckett Road and Oxford Street routes opened in 1903, with the Brodsworth route commencing in 1916. A short service, prior to the construction of the North Bridge, from Frenchgate to Marshgate, also started in 1902 to link the town centre with the Bentley route which at the time finished at a point north of the Great Northern Railway Company's level crossing.

The Corporation began services in 1902 with fifteen cars obtained from Dick Kerr and Co. of Preston. There were open top fifty-six seaters with reversed staircases, and mounted on Brill 21E trucks. A further ten cars were purchased in 1903 together with a water car/snow broom and a 'salt and sand' trailer, the latter having been rebuilt from a York horse-car.

The trams operating on the Bentley route were housed in a large shed built by the Corporation in Marshgate whilst all the other vehicles used the car shed in Greyfriars Road.

During the years preceding the First World War the Bentley tram terminus was moved to Frenchgate, following the completion of the North Bridge, which allowed the trams to travel through to the town centre. Also, cross-town services were introduced, linking Balby to Beckett Road and Hexthorpe to Avenue Road. The appearance of the trams changed in 1913 as some of the cars were provided with covers over the top decks. This followed the purchase earlier in the year of six vehicles already incorporating covered top decks.

Due to the shortage of manpower following the outbreak of the First World War, the trams were staffed almost entirely by women. Additions to the tram network in the war years included the extension of the Balby route to Warmsworth in 1915 and the introduction of a Brodsworth route in 1916 which ran for much of the way on the grass margin alongside the Great North Road. The Corporation purchased four new cars from Dick Kerr and Co. to commence this latter service and these were direct stairs balcony cars seating sixty-six passengers. In the early 1920s an extension to the Greyfriars Road tram shed was built and ten more cars were purchased, these being the only trams in Doncaster to have enclosed platforms.

Gradually, however, the trams suffered increasing competition from motorbuses, and even converted vans and covered lorries operating unscheduled services along the tram routes. A serious fall in receipts coupled with an increasing problem of track deterioration led the Corporation to make several far-reaching decisions. They not only decided to abolish plans to extend the network to Hatfield, Rossington and Armthorpe, but also to gradually eliminate all tram services. They intended instead to obtain the necessary powers to operate motorbuses and trolleybuses. The Avenue Road tram route was the first to close in 1925, being replaced by motorbuses on an experimental basis. The Bentley route closed in 1928, with the Hexthorpe and Beckett Road routes closing in 1929, the Racecourse and Hyde Park routes in 1930 and the Balby route in 1931. The last tram to run in Doncaster was on the Brodsworth route on the 8 June 1935. Eventually all these routes, with the exception of Brodsworth, were replaced by trolleybus services, whilst the Brodsworth and all new routes were served by motorbuses.

The first operational trolley service ran on the Bentley route on the 22 August 1928 from a new bus stand built on North Bridge. The Corporation purchased four vehicles from Garretts of Leiston and four from Karriers of Luton (all three-axle vehicles) to begin the service. In due course, as the tram fleet diminished, a further twenty-two similar Karrier vehicles were obtained. These thirty vehicles, together with one especially built for the Corporation by the Bristol Bus Company, were the only type to be bought in which the top deck did not extend over the driver's cab.

Although trolleys still made use of the Greyfriars Road depot, the main terminus in Station Road was abandoned. It was decided there would be too much congestion in this location so a terminus for each trolley route was found elsewhere.

The Second World War had little effect on trolleybus services since they ran normally throughout the day, but terminated at 9.30 p.m. During the war years there were two extensions made to the existing trolley routes. The Beckett Road route was extended for about a half mile along Beckett Road in April 1941, and the Balby route extended along Warmsworth Road to Barrel Lane in July 1942.

New trolleys purchased in the 1930s were all three-axle sixty seaters. By the early 1940s the original batch of trolleys needed replacement, and in 1943 Doncaster acquired its first two-axle fifty-six seater. Other groups of two-axle trolleybuses were subsequently obtained, in most cases second-hand from other companies as the need to replace the three-axle vehicles occurred. Fourteen three-axle trolleys were withdrawn in 1955 as a result of the closure of the Bentley service. In this year building work commenced to replace the Mill Bridge over the River Don, and as it was envisaged that this would take a considerable time to complete a decision was taken to convert the Bentley route to motorbus operation. The remaining three-axle vehicles were withdrawn in 1957, one in July and the last two during September.

Two final developments in the trolleybus system occurred in 1958. One was a further extension of a half mile along the Beckett Road route and the second was an extension of a quarter mile along Thorne Road on the Wheatley Hills route. The trolley network was, perhaps inevitably, gradually abandoned. It became superseded by the expanding and increasingly complex urban layout of the 1960s, and an escalating dominance of motorised transport, which was able to adapt more successfully to changing times.

ONE

Avenue Road and Wheatley Hills

Car no. 18, shortly after being purchased in 1903, at the junction of Town Moor Avenue and Thorne Road. This type of tramcar provided no protection for the driver or conductor against the weather. On extremely cold winter mornings, if no passengers were being carried some drivers and conductors, leaving the tram to operate independently, jogged alongside the vehicle in an effort to keep warm. In 1927 nos 18 and 3 were withdrawn and sold off as garden sheds. The Corporation's original tramway plans specified the system would be operated with single deck trams, but instead small, standard-designed, two-axle 'open-top' trams were acquired; many other towns had similar vehicles. In this photograph the driver's controls are clearly seen on the front platform. The first handle is the handbrake and the second is the speed controller; between them is a small reversing key. On the floor there was a pedal to provide sand for use on greasy rails and another to sound a warning gong.

John G. Steadman, a native of Lincolnshire, commenced running local horse bus services in 1887. Amongst the services he operated was a regular daily cross-town service between Hyde Park and Avenue Road. The journeys took a quarter of an hour from the town centre terminus – the Market place – to each 'outer' terminus. Later, as Station Road became recognised as the centre of town traffic, Steadman introduced a service from Station Road to Avenue Road. It commenced at 8.00 a.m. each morning and continued a half hourly service until 8.30 p.m. The photograph of the Avenue Road to Station Road single horse bus was taken at the fountain in Station Road.

The Avenue Road and Beckett Road tram routes shared the same track as far as the junction at Broxholme Lane. From there the Avenue Road route continued along Highfield Road, turned right at King's Road and then followed Thorne Road to the terminus at the 'southern end' of Avenue Road. The Avenue Road tram services operated from 8.00 a.m. to 10.12 p.m. Both outward and return journeys took approx. 12 minutes though the service was underutilised with some journeys attracting only two or three people. Car no. 11 is approaching Baxter Gate on its return journey from Avenue Road.

The short Avenue Road route was opened on 15 January 1903. Five other Corporations in South Yorkshire and Humberside established tram services around this time and these were, Sheffield and Hull in 1899, Grimsby in 1901, Barnsley in 1902, Rotherham in 1903 and Mexborough/Swinton in 1907. Car no. 25 passes the splendid edifice of the Corn Exchange on its way to the Station Road terminus.

Car no. 14 is in King's Road on the return journey to the town centre. An affluent area like King's Road and indeed Thorne Road was not ideal territory for trams because the population density was low and people used other means of transport. Thus the Avenue Road service was uneconomical for much of its life. In an attempt to reduce costs a small single-deck tram was bought second hand from Erith, near London, in 1916. Known as a demi-car it was intended to be one-man operated, but due to union objections a conductor was retained, which defeated the object of having a smaller car.

View, facing north, of the King's Road section of the Avenue Road tramway route. Initially the Corporation's plans included a line to Avenue Road via Baxter Gate, the Market area, Copley Road and Broxholme Lane. However due to protests from market traders, Sunny Bar and Netherhall Road were used instead of the Market area and Copley Road.

This shows much of the Thorne Road section of the of the Avenue Road tram route. Beyond the terminus at this time, there was nothing more than fields and farm buildings. After trams were withdrawn from the service in 1925 they were replaced by motorbuses on an experimental basis; the route was also extended along Thorne Road into the new estates under construction at Wheatley Hills. Motorbuses were subsequently replaced by trolleybuses in 1931.

An Avenue Road tram is seen at speed on leaving the outer terminus. Doncaster and Hull's electric tramway systems were quite different from any other in the country because they employed 'centre grooved' rails. Doncaster's tracks differed from those at Hull in one respect however, since instead of being laid on a wooden pavement they were housed in concrete, a factor that contributed to the system's early demise.

Car no. 11, at the Avenue Road outer terminus, was fitted with a top deck cover and direct staircase by the Dick Kerr and Co. in 1913, becoming a balcony car. All the rebuilt cars could be easily distinguished from the later newly built balcony cars by the fact that rebuilt cars end destination boxes were mounted in the lower saloon, whilst new cars had them in the upper saloon.

Car no. 6 threads its way along St Sepulchre Gate on route to the town centre terminus in Station Road. In tramway days, there was only room for a single track, which was insufficient for a section of the system used by several tram car services. Car no. 6 was fitted with a top deck cover and direct staircase by Brush in 1913, becoming a balcony car. Cars 6-15 were withdrawn in 1930 and sold to Mr Buxton (dealer and breaker) Tickhill Road, Doncaster. Most of the cars were broken up but some were sold as garden sheds.

The view taken in the 1920s in Station Road features a bus on the right, working on the Wheatley Hills service which was introduced to replace and extend the Avenue Road tramway during April 1925. This was Doncaster's first tramway route closure and the first Corporation motorbus service wholly within the borough boundary. It was also the first time double-decked buses were used. Initially the vehicles were unable to cope with the passenger loads and a tram was sometimes used on Avenue Road at peak periods.

On the whole trolleybuses were very popular with the public, as they provided a smooth and comfortable ride in comparison with earlier trams and motorbuses. A trolleybus working on the Thorne Road section of the Wheatley Hills route passes the Green House (later Cumberland) Hotel. The Wheatley Hills route was favoured by trolleybus drivers since it followed a relatively straight course; the outward and return journeys being completed quite easily in the allotted time.

Karrier 'E6' D/D trolleybus no. 355 was part of a batch, fleet nos 49-68, acquired in 1939 and that were renumberd 349-368 in 1947. Trolleybus no. 355 is near the Doncaster Royal Infirmary whilst returning to the town centre on 30 January 1955, which was only six months before its withdrawal from service. During November 1955 vehicle nos 354-356 went to Max Speed Transportation Co., Surrey, for scrap.

Trolleybuses and motorbuses operating in Doncaster's narrow town-centre streets became a hindrance to each other from the outset, but the Corporation, through accepting the national trend of motorbus introduction during the 1920s, did not want to rely solely on this mode of transport because of its high operating costs and the short life expectancy of the vehicles used. Trolleybuses on the other hand, could continue to utilise power from the electricity station, and as the life span and reliability of these vehicles was higher than that of motorbuses, both forms of transport were retained in Doncaster and co-existed for over 30 years. The trolley is at Wheatley Hotel on the turning circle.

The junction at Thorne Road and Barnby Dun Road near the Wheatley Hills outer terminus provided a suitable location for a 'turning circle'. Sometimes however, during thick fog, drivers found it difficult to anticipate the circle and overran the wires, becoming stranded on Barnby Dun Road. The extension of the route from the 'Wheatley Hotel' to Sandall Park which was opened 14 October 1958 was the last addition to Doncaster's trolleybus network. Trolleybuses ceased to operate on the Wheatley Hills route on 30 December 1962. Trolleybus no. 385 was photographed at the Wheatley Hills terminus on 30 April 1955.

Trolleybus no. 391 on Thorne Road, 8 April 1955. This is a 1945 ex-Southend-on Sea-'W' D/D trolleybus acquired by Doncaster in 1954 having a Park Royal utility H30/26R body. It was also in a batch 385-392 that was temporarily withdrawn in 1957-8, the chassis overhauled, and then rebodied by Roe's.

Trolleybus no. 392 on turning circle at Sandall Park. The vehicle's Utility body went to Martin (breaker), Toll Bar, Doncaster in June 1958 and following withdrawal in June 1962, the chassis went to Bolland (breaker), Wakefield. The Roe body was fitted by Roe's to a new Daimler motorbus chassis fleet no. 173.

17

Karrier/Sunbeam 'W' D/D utility trolleybus no. 377 at the town centre terminus outside Hodgson & Hepworth's store. This vehicle was one of a batch of three Karrier/Sunbeam 'W' D/D utility trolleybuses with Park Royal H30/26R bodies acquired in 1945. They were fleet nos 75-77 but renumbered 375-377 in 1947. They were painted all-over chocolate livery until 1946, and rebodied by Roe's in 1955. No. 377 was repillared and panelled in 1948 and withdrawn from service in December 1963.

Karrier/Sunbeam 'W' D/D trolleybus no. 374 passes the Cleveland Street/Wood Street junction on its way to the town centre terminus. Acquired in 1945 and out of service, being rebodied between October 1954 and February 1955, the vehicle was withdrawn during October 1963 and sold for scrap in the following year.

TWO
Balby and Warmsworth

Car no. 6 is working on the Balby-Becket Road cross-town service. This was one of two such services introduced in 1904 the other being Avenue Road to Hexthorpe. One of the reasons was to avoid congestion caused by conductors changing the trolley boom's direction in the centre of the town's narrow streets. However the cross town services were not very effective because of uneven loads on some sections of the routes – particularly on the Avenue Road stretch.

A horse bus service operated by local grocery and provision merchants Hodgson & Hepworth's is seen at Balby. The company's main aim was to convey customers, from the outlying villages, to their large store in St Sepulchre Gate. Noted amongst the other local horse bus operators were J. G. Steadman and J. Stoppani. It is also worth mentioning that Doncaster Corporation abandoned the idea of horse-drawn tramway system in 1878.

The first fifteen trams arrived by rail from Dick Kerr of Preston in 1902, reaching the Shakespeare Dock yard at the foot of Hexthorpe Bridge and being assembled on their wheels at the depot soon after arrival. Car no. 4 has just passed the YMCA building in St Sepulchre Gate on its way to the town centre. The car was a fifty-six seater (34/22) with reversed stairs and was one of only a few not fitted with a top deck cover, being withdrawn in 1927.

Station Road was only twenty years old when it was utilised as a tram terminus in 1902. From St Sepulchre Gate it formed a new approach to the railway station and contained many impressive buildings. The Balby tram route was double tracked to the Shakespeare's Head Hotel, except for a short distance at the junction with the Hexthorpe route. The remainder of the route was single track, with passing loops at the Balby Steam Laundry, Carr View, Burton Avenue and Balby Church. When the route was extended to Warmsworth there were 'passing loops' at Oswin Avenue, Anelay Road, Barrel Lane, the White House and Quaker Lane. The photograph of car no. 14 was taken by Luke Bagshaw prior to the vehicle being fitted, in 1913, with a top deck cover and a direct staircase.

Passengers are disembarking from car no. 16 before it moves to the Station Road terminus, a short distance past the Glyn Temperance Hotel. All the 'open top' trams had 'reversed stairs' which often obstructed the driver's left hand side view. The tramway staff are wearing uniforms with 'pill-box' hats supplied by the Doncaster Co-operative Society; the first set incorporated a yellow trim, but two years later it was changed to red.

Tram services to Balby began at 5.00 a.m. When the route was extended from Oswin Avenue (Balby) to Warmsworth, the passengers travelling on the early morning services included miners on their way to the Yorkshire Main Colliery at Edlington. On reaching Warmsworth the miners walked the remainder of their journey. Car no. 14 is on the St Sepulchre Gate section of the Balby route.

The tram at the rear in this picture is waiting for car no. 19 to enter a section of double track so that the two vehicles may pass. The picture may have been taken around 1903 when Doncaster Corporation attempted to recoup their losses on the tramways and allow external advertisements on the trams, each vehicle being 'let' for £21 per annum. Slogans had to be painted on the cream panels surrounding the top deck, in the same red as the rest of the tram. The YMCA building on the right has since been demolished yet a number of buildings on the thoroughfare still remain albeit in a dilapidated state.

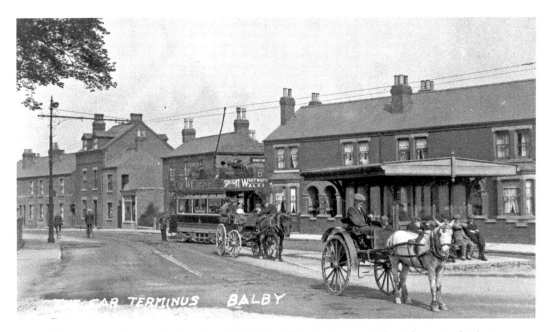

The tram terminus at the junction of High Road/Oswin Avenue, Balby. The car is displaying the route letter 'B', signifying that it was operating on the cross-town service between Beckett Road and Balby. The tracks ended in a 'Y' arrangement (a characteristic feature of Doncaster tramways) on either side of the tram shelter.

The tram terminus building was locked at certain times to restrict vandalism and was eventually removed. On 4 February 1915 the Balby route was extended to Warmsworth.

Car no. 12 glides past Green Field Lane with Low Road to the right. The Balby line ran for some distance into the area of Balby-with-Hexthorpe Urban District, which was only absorbed into Doncaster during 1914. The route was part of a five mile tramway scheme proposed by the British Electric Traction Company in 1898. This firm was formed to acquire or build electric tramways throughout the country. Its only success in South Yorkshire was at Barnsley, where its tramway later formed the nucleus of the Yorkshire Traction Bus Company.

Tram pausing adjacent to Fisher's Park (obscured by the tall trees on the left) for a passenger to board the vehicle. The chairman of the Tramways Committee was Councillor George Smith, who was from Retford and began his career with Hodgson & Hepworths in St Sepulchre Gate. Later he bought the mineral water business of a Mr Heath who had died, and cemented the union by marrying the deceased's eldest daughter becoming the firm of Heath & Smith whose business premises were not far away from the location here.

The Warmsworth tram terminus was initially situated outside the Cecil & Battie Wrightson Arms public house but in 1919 a short spur was constructed along Edlington Lane, after which time cars stopped adjacent to the Co-operative Society's building. This new section was fitted with the only 'trolley reverser' on the system. The conductors on nearly all the other routes had to change the trolley manually. When the Warmsworth tram route was replaced by the trolleybus operation, passengers living on the section between Austen Avenue, Balby and Warmsworth, which was not served by trolleybuses, had to use the Edlington motorbus service.

The tram's route indicator in the photograph here, as well as denoting the vehicle is working on the cross-town service to Beckett Road, helps to date the picture – sometime between 1915 (when the Warmsworth extension opened) and 1917 when cross town services ceased. The failure to extend the route as far as Edlington encouraged private motorbus competition and the Corporation was forced into running its Edlington motorbus service from 1923. Receipts on the route fell drastically from £5,500 per annum in 1923 to £1,100 in 1930 with only £78 11s 0d being taken during the last week of tram services.

Scene outside the Cecil & Battie Wrightson Arms with a tram working on a cross-town service to Beckett Road.

Workers attending to track in St Sepulchre Gate used by the Balby and Hexthorpe trams.

Dick Kerr tram no. 5 on Warmsworth Road.

Car no. 43 passes the Good Woman Inn and the Crystal Palace Inn on the left as it makes its way to Warmsworth. This tram is a Dick Kerr sixty-six seat (40/26) vestibule balcony car and was in the fleet, nos 38-47, acquired in 1920. Mounted on 8 foot 6 inch Peckham P22 trucks these were the only trams in Doncaster to have enclosed platforms. No. 43 survived until withdrawal in June 1935 and may have been broken up along with others at the Greyfriars Road depot before going to Mr Buxton (dealer and breaker), Tickhill, Road, Doncaster.

During the First World War as large numbers of the male population joined the fighting abroad, women became employed for the first time in a variety of jobs, including both tram driving and conducting. Here the female crew of car no. 27 take a rest from their duties and pose at Oswin Avenue, in 1917. Every car was 'blacked out' during the evenings in anticipation of Zeppelin attacks, and warnings of imminent raids were given by the electricity station dimming all tram lights three times. After much discussion and disagreement Sunday services were introduced in 1914. These operated from noon to 9.00 p.m.

Belonging to the batch of 10 trams purchased in 1920, car no. 42, a vestibuled balcony vehicle, passes Tenter Road and Quaker Lane on its way to the Warmsworth outer terminus. Much road widening on this section of the Doncaster – Sheffield A630 route has taken place in the intervening years.

Vestibuled balcony cars numbered 40 and 42 are seen together on a 'passing loop' at Oswin Avenue, Balby on the last day of tram operation on the route, 25 July 1931. Car no. 40 was the last tram to run in Doncaster on 8 June 1935 and, without a farewell ceremony, the system was closed after thirty-three years of service. The life-span for other systems in South Yorkshire ranged from nine years of operation by the Dearne District Light Railways to sixty-one years by the Sheffield Corporation.

Although the tram terminus at Balby was abandoned in 1915 a service continued to operate to Balby, mainly at busy times. On the last day of tram operation on the route, car no. 46 is leaving Oswin Avenue carrying only a few passengers. This car along with the nine others purchased in 1920, were amongst the only ones fitted with 'hinged' seats that could be 'folded up' to make the cleaners' awkward task of sweeping the floors less arduous and time consuming.

The Balby route became the busiest trolleybus service. Six vehicles usually operated on the route during weekdays with ten on Saturdays. Trolleybus crews often complained that 12 minutes allowed for the outward journey and 13 minutes for the return was impracticable since the route was very busy and there were sixteen stops to make. Initially the Balby trolleybus route only extended as far as Austen Avenue into which trolleys turned to use a reverser. Karrier 'E6' D/D trolleybuses 27 and 28 pass one another near Oswin Avenue, on the first day of trolleybus operation on the Balby route, 26 July 1931. These vehicles belong to a batch of seven trolleybuses acquired in 1931, fleet nos 24-30., registered nos DT 3153-DT 3159. These were the last D/Ds delivered to Doncaster, where the top deck did not extend over the cab. They also had the front destination boxes built into the cab roof instead of into the windscreen. Nos 27 and 28 were withdrawn in June 1939. After being taken out of service nos 25 and 28 were stored at Leicester Avenue depot until December 1944, as possible replacements for war damaged vehicles.

Trolleybus no. 359 at the town centre terminus in West Laith Gate. Trolleybus services operated on the Balby route from 4.36 a.m., the earliest trolleybus to begin services travelled down St Sepulchre Gate on the 'wrong' side of the road. As there were no wires to lead the vehicle into West Laith Gate, the conductor and an inspector used 'trolley' poles to pull the trolleys off the wires, allowing the vehicle to 'free wheel' to the terminus. Here the trolleys were attached to the route wires. Later, as other vehicles began services, they made a long detour along the Racecourse route and changed on to the Balby wires at Jacobs' Corner. In later years to avoid these unorthodox manoeuvres and lengthy detours, a short length of wiring was extended from St Sepulchre Gate across to West Laith Gate.

Karrier 'E6' D/D trolleybus no. 357 is at the St Sepulchre Gate/Cleveland Street junction on 10 July 1955. The vehicle, with a Roe H32/28R body, Metrovic electrical gear and 80 hp motor, was bought in a batch of twenty in 1939, fleet nos 49-68, later renumbered 349-368, 1947. They were registered nos BDT 114-129 and BDT 131-134 and withdrawn between 1954-1957.

Karrier 'E6' D/D trolley no. 362 in St Sepulchre Gate West passing Ganter's shop c. 1955. This vehicle was loaned to Rotherham Corporation Transport for clearance tests (prior to their conversion to D/D trolleybus operation) on 19 June 1955.

Trolleybus in a tangle at the Balby Road/Kelham Street junction. Student trolleybus conductor Michael Fowler recalls: 'The long bamboo pole used to flick the trolleyheads from wire to wire ... was housed in a long tube under the bus, although when it was in frequent use on journeys to and from the depot it was propped on the platform at an angle of sixty degrees from the front of the platform bulkhead to the rear handrail.'

Balby trolleybus returning to the town centre where the Alma Hotel can be seen in the distance on the right, 15 May 1955. A proposal announced in 1958 for a trolleybus route to extend from the Balby route to Broomhouse Lane was dismissed in favour of motorbus operation.

Karrier 'E6' D/D trolleybus no. 356 approaching Balby Bridge on 30 June 1955. On his website www.petergould.co.uk, transport historian Peter Gould states: 'The original design of Karrier-Clough vehicles were developed from the six-wheeled double-deck Karrier WL6/2 motorbus chassis, and was designated the E6. A new series of chassis numbers was commenced at 54001 (although the first vehicles delivered, to Doncaster Corporation in 1928 had chassis numbers 54003-54006). A total of 44 Karrier-Clough trolleybuses were sold, mainly going to Doncaster Corporation, although Derby, Nottingham and York Corporations all had examples'.

Trolleybus no. 365 displaying the Balby route number ten passes the Steam Laundry, now demolished, in Balby Road on 24 September 1955. The mileage covered on the Balby route was 2.25.

The driver and conductor of trolleybus no. 351 at Barrel Lane, Warmsworth. Sometimes during the autumn months the trolleybus crews, with the aid of a 'trolley pole', would assist the local youngsters to obtain 'conkers' from a Horse Chestnut tree nearby. This vehicle is a rebodied 1944 Karrier/Sunbeam 'W' D/D trolleybus with 1957 Roe H34/28R body, and was purchased second hand along with no. 352 in 1957 from Pontypridd Urban District Council. They were Pontypridd nos 10 and 11. After trouble in towing no. 11 from Pontypridd, the top deck of no. 10 was removed in Pontypridd before towing it to Doncaster on 1 February 1957. The bottom deck of no. 10 and the complete utility body of no. 11 were removed and sold to Martin (breaker) Toll Bar, near Doncaster, in February 1957. The chassis were then overhauled by DCT before the Roe bodies were fitted. No. 35 had its English electric 85 hp motor and automatic acceleration gear replaced by conventional Metrovic 85 hp motor and gear in 1960. This vehicle was the hundredth trolleybus purchased by DCT.

One of the difficulties of trolleybus operation was providing suitable facilities for the vehicles to turn round at the end of each journey. For the first eleven years of trolleybus operation on the Balby route the trolleys were turned by means of a 'turning triangle'. When the terminus was moved to Barrel Lane in 1942 a more practical 'turning circle' was utilised. The six wheel vehicle in this photograph is demonstrating how the manoeuvre was achieved. It was said that the local outcry against the extension was great, as it was feared that the buses would be filled up on setting out by Edlington miners in their 'pit muck', who had walked from Yorkshire Main Colliery. In the event, very few miners appeared, having their own motor bus 'specials'.

THREE

Beckett Road

On a busy afternoon, car no. 13 is pictured in St Sepulchre gate, whilst working on a cross town service. Note the tramway inspector's hut in the foreground. This tram was in the batch of 15 vehicles nos 1-15 purchased in 1902. It was fitted with a top deck cover by the Dick Kerr and Co. in 1913 and withdrawn seventeen years later. Dick Kerr and Co. was a locomotive and tramcar manufacturer based in Kilmarnock, Scotland and Preston, England. Having previously been known as W. B. Dick and Company the company had built all kinds of tramway equipment and rolling stock. From 1883 the company joined with John Kerr and under its new name, it built around fifty locomotives up to 1919. Until the late 1890s the company had largely produced steam tramway engines, but soon afterwards it became one of the largest manufacturers of electric tramway cars. The company facilities in Preston were acquired in 1893 along with the railway and tramway plant activities of Hartley, Arnoux and Fanning who had been bought out by Kerr Stuart and Company.

The Beckett Road tram route was single-tracked. There were 'passing loops' at the Corn Exchange, Nether Hall Road and Holmes Market; the terminus was at the 'north end' of Avenue Road. This tram is working on a cross-town service between Beckett Road and Balby.

Scene at the junction of Broxholme Lane and Highfield Road which was where the Beckett Road and Avenue Road trams parted company on the way to their respective destinations.

View along Broxholme Lane with a tram in the distance; Copley Road is to the left. The Beckett Road tramway route opened in 1903.

Scene at the Beckett Road outer terminus near Morley Road where the tram conductor is adjusting the trolley boom to enable the vehicle to return to the town centre.

The passing loop in Nether Hall Road with the Broxholme Lane Methodist Church to the right. Tram drivers' instructions stated: 'In passing places of Worship on the Sabbath, the use of the gong (i.e. the tramcar's equivalent of a horn) must be restricted as much as possible, and the car run slowly.'

The conductor and driver of car no. 9 in Nether Hall Road. This vehicle was in the first fifteen trams, fleet nos 1-15, purchased in 1902. The photograph is pre-1913 when nos 5-9 were fitted with top deck covers and direct staircases by Brush, becoming balcony cars.

Another section of the Nether Hall Road tram route is seen here with Russell Terrace to the left.

Car no. 13 approaches the busy Clock Corner junction on its return to the town centre. Once again we see a tram that was acquired in the original batch of fifteen trams in 1902. This picture is after 1913 when a top deck cover and a direct staircase was added by Dick Kerr and Co. Nos 6-15 were withdrawn in 1930.

During the early years of trolleybus operations on the Beckett Road route (service no. 5) vehicles were turned round at the 'outer' terminus in Wentworth Road by means of a 'turning triangle'. Drivers of the early Garrett and Karrier trolleybuses, like no. 16 at Wentworth Road, *c.* 1930, often complained that the cab roof leaked when it rained heavily and that the small headlamps gave poor visibility.

Karrier 'E6' D/D trolleybus no. 16 with a Roe H32/28R body, BTH electrical gear and a 60 hp motor was acquired in a batch of six vehicles fleet nos 11-16 in 1929. No. 16 was in service from July 1929 until 30 April 1945. The entire batch of 1929 trolleys was sold to a Mr Buxton for scrap as follows, no. 11, 7 June 1939, nos 12, 14 and 15 December 1944, no. 13, 14 August 1939 and no. 16, 16 August 1945.

An aerial view of a Beckett Road or Wheatley Hills trolley returning to the town centre terminus. For part of the journey on the Wheatley Hills service wires were shared with the Beckett Road service, and in order not to cause any confusion between the two routes on one common section 'Wheatley Hills' was printed in red on the destination blinds.

Karrier 'E6' D/D trolleybus no. 48 in Nether Hall Road whilst returning to the town centre. Michael Fowler a student trolleybus conductor in the mid-1950s recalls: 'I discovered ... how the driver changed the points on the overhead wires. It was very simple really. At a specified location just before the junction he would draw power with the accelerator pedal at an automatic 'frog' in the wires or just coast over it, depending on which direction he intended to take.' No. 48 was acquired in a batch of six vehicles, fleet nos 43-8, during 1938, was renumbered 348 in 1947 and withdrawn on 26 February 1955.

Karrier 'E6' D/D trolleybus no. 344 approaches the Beckett Road/Avenue Road junction *c.* 1955. After arriving in 1938 with a Roe H32/28R body, the vehicle was renumbered from no. 44 to 344 in 1947 and in service until 23 March 1955. After withdrawal nos 43-45 (later 343-5) went to Max Speed Transportation Co. (dealers), Swains Road, Mitcham, Surrey, for scrap in November 1955. Charles H. Roe Ltd. was a Yorkshire coachbuilding company. It was reformed in 1923 (after the 1921 company failed) based at Crossgates Carriage Works, in Leeds. Then in 1947 was taken over by Park Royal Vehicles, two years later along with parent company Park Royal Vehicles, it became part of Associated Commercial Vehicles (ACV) in 1949, which was merged with Leyland Motors Ltd in 1962. The Charles H. Roe company closed in 1984. In the following year, a group of employees from the former business, supported by Yorkshire Enterprise Ltd, began the Optare coachbuilding business in the former Roe carriage works.

Karrier/Sunbeam 'W' D/D utility trolleybus no. 377 with a Park Royal H30/26R body passes the Corn Exchange (left) whilst moving steadily through the busy Market Place. Sunbeam was born when John Marston, a manufacturer of tin plate and Japan ware, produced the first Sunbeam bicycle in 1887. Later cars and motorcycles were produced. In 1931 Sunbeam Commercial Vehicles was formed and their standard six-wheeled chassis, made at Moorfield Road works were built into a trolleybus. This was an immediate success, large numbers were produced and Sunbeam eventually became one of the world's leading bus chassis manufacturers.

The Beckett Road terminus was the only terminal point which involved dropping off the last passengers and turning round. On all other routes passengers were on the vehicle at all times. A former trolleybus conductor recalled the following: 'Later on in my conducting career – with certain drivers – I had to find out exactly what time the films [at the Astra] ended and be prepared to be very quick on the bell as soon as the doors were flung open, much to the annoyance of the first people out. The rest did not see us anyway, because acceleration was, to say the least, very rapid. One person who did not cotton on of course, was the driver of the following trolleybus, but he had probably done the same thing to our driver a few weeks previously.' Here, trolleybus no. 353 passes the Astra Cinema on the left on its way to the outer terminus.

Karrier/Sunbeam 'W' D/D trolleybus no. 373 is outside the Astra Cinema on 1 February 1955. The vehicle was bought in a batch of three in 1945, fleet nos 72-74, renumbered 372-373, 1947. The batch was painted battleship grey with one white band under lower saloon windows until 1946. The vehicles were all temporarily withdrawn, the chassis overhauled and rebodied H34/28R by Roes – 373 was out of service 5 July 1954 until 31 December 1954, and finally withdrawn on 15 October 1963. Trolleybus nos 372, 373, 374, 376 and 377 all went to Bolland (breaker), Wakefield during February 1964 for scrap.

Karrier 'E6' D/D trolleybus no. 348 in Printing Office Street. We saw this vehicle on page 41 as no. 48.

Sunbeam 'W' D/D trolleybus no. 391 has just turned off from Nether Hall Road on to Broxholme Lane on 1 April 1959. The vehicle was acquired in 1954 in a batch of eight, fleet nos 385-392. They were all temporarily withdrawn, 391 from 23 February 1958 until 1 September 1958, for rebodying by Roe's. No. 391 was withdrawn on 22 July 1962, the Utility body went to Martin, March 1958, chassis to Bolland and the Roe body to a new Daimler motorbus chassis fleet no. 182.

Karrier 'E6' D/D trolleybus no. 348 near the Beckett Road/Avenue Road junction on 12 Feb 1955. At this time the vehicle was only two weeks away from withdrawal on 26 February 1955 after being in service since 12 July 1938.

Karrier/Sunbeam 'W' D/D utility trolleybus no. 375 in Holmes Market c. 1955. This vehicle has been at Sandtoft Transport Centre since November 1969.

The overhead points in Nether Hall Road, at the junction of the Beckett Road and Wheatley Hills routes, were permanently set for the Beckett Road trolleybus to turn left down Broxholme Lane. The Beckett Road driver, however, to ensure he did not change the points had to 'drift' without 'drawing' power under a magnetic switch just before the junction. Conversely the Wheatley Hills driver had to ensure that he was 'drawing' power when he travelled under the switch since this was the only way the points could be changed to allow him to travel straight ahead. Once the Wheatley Hills driver had travelled over the junction another mechanism was triggered to reset the points. Two workmen from the maintenance section are pictured with the overhead tower wagon investigating a fault on the system.

A six-wheeled trolleybus at the Beckett Road outer terminus on 25 September 1955.

Above and below: Work taking place on the final extension to the Beckett Road trolleybus route, which was opened on 17 February 1958.

Another view of Karrier/Sunbeam 'W' D/D utility trolleybus no. 375 at Beckett Road outer terminus. The mileage covered on the Beckett Road route was 2.01.

Karrier/Sunbeam 'W' D/D trolleybus no. 373 rounds a corner at the Corn Exchange on 29 April 1962. The vehicle had around eighteen months of service left, being withdrawn on 15 October 1963.

A rebodied 1943 Sunbeam trolleybus no. 398 at the Broxholme Lane/Nether Hall Road junction on 29 October 1962. This vehicle was acquired in 1955 in a batch of six, fleet nos 393-398. The chassis of these six vehicles, complete with Brush utility B35C bodies, were purchased second hand from the Mexborough & Swinton Traction Co. in February 1955. They were Mexborough & Swinton nos 1-6. The S/D bodies were removed and sold to Martin (breaker) Toll bar, near Doncaster, and the chassis overhauled by DCT before the 1955 Roe D/D bodies were fitted.

The 1960s revealed a fundamental re-thinking of Doncaster Corporation's public transport policy; its aims for economy and efficiency, amidst wide-ranging town centre redevelopment, inevitably led to a serious appraisal of the future of electric transport in the area. Coupled with an inherent inflexibility, the expense of re-wiring for the new trolleybus routes cast serious doubts over the long term future of this form of public transport. Trolleybus no. 375 in St Sepulchre Gate on the last day of trolleybus operations 14 December 1963.

The last trolley at Beckett Road 14 December 1963, no. 375 (CDT 636) a 1945 Karrier/ Sunbeam 'W' D/D with its 1950s Roe body. And sixty-one years of electric transport in Doncaster ended in 1963 when no. 375 operated that final commemorative run along the Beckett Road route. At 7.30 p.m. as the trolley began its last journey, a familiar and well-liked feature of Doncaster town life was about to end. It is recalled today by surviving photographs which, intentional or otherwise, caught in time a townscape and its transport system no description or memory can ever make permanent. No. 375 is preserved at Sandtoft Trolleybus Museum near Doncaster.

FOUR

Bentley

Car no. 11 displaying the Bentley route sign in the window was purchased in 1902. Initially Doncaster Corporation hoped to run trams over the G.N.R's East Coast Main Line using the level crossing but the company turned down the request. This meant the Bentley trams began services on the west side of the line. On commencement of the Bentley service on 27 October 1903 a 'shuttle service' was organised from Station Road to the French Gate side of the level crossing. But this was under used and withdrawn. Undeterred, the Corporation tried another feeder service which operated at weekends from the Guildhall to the level crossing. This too was unsuccessful only running for around two months.

Car no. 12 is captured just before disappearing over the Mill Bridge on its return journey to the town centre. Until 1910 the Bentley tram services began in Marsh Gate and cars were housed in a shed built in the area. The shed, accommodating around three or four vehicles, collapsed during a gale around 1904 and was replaced.

Car no. 7 is moving along Bentley Road. Tram nos 7 and 14 were retrucked with 7 foot Peckham P22 trucks in 1921. The picture is pre-1913 when the vehicle was fitted with a top deck cover and direct staircase, becoming a balcony car.

Car no. 11 near St Peters Church (out of view on the right).

Two cars nos 7 and 12 using the passing loop on Bentley Road. Both vehicles were fitted with top deck covers and direct staircases in 1913. The Bentley route contained seven passing loops.

Car no. 14 is just entering Bentley Road with Yarbrough Terrace to the right. Bentley having its own Urban District Council tussled with Doncaster Council in 1915 over the tram track's condition stating it was 'deplorable and dangerous.'

An unidentified tram (possibly no. 6) dodges other road traffic near the bridge spanning the Doncaster-Leeds railway line.

Before the opening of the North Bridge, trams had to begin services on the west side of the level crossing, where a tram is just visible in the picture here.

This photograph was taken during the First World War, an observation confirmed by the presence of the female crew and the tram's headlamp mask, a precaution against Zeppelin raids. Coupled with the difficulty of staffing the trams during the War was the additional problem of maintaining them due to the dearth of skilled labour. The vehicle here has most likely been involved in several collisions and some emergency repairs to hold the body together have involved three large bolts being placed in the rocker panel, just below the fleet name.

Dick Kerr car no. 24, belongs to a batch of five vehicles, fleet nos 21-25, that were acquired in 1904. It is displaying the New Village [Bentley] route indicator while staff pose proudly for the camera. On 20 March 1913 the Bentley route was extended along The Avenue in New Village to within a short distance of the colliery which was more convenient for miners travelling to and from work; the pit obviously having boosted passenger traffic on the route. Prior to the extension colliers had to trek from the original terminus in Bentley High Street to the pit. The picture is post 1913 when the vehicle was fitted with a top deck cover and direct staircase by Dick Kerr and Co. Car nos 23 and 24 were re-trucked with 7 foot 6 inch Peckham trucks in 1922.

This is the original Bentley High street tram terminus which included a section of track leading into Chapel Street so that the trams would not obstruct other traffic in the main road. In 1907 the Corporation bought four top deck covers after seeing Sheffield's trams fitted with them. By 1913 sixteen of the 'older cars', like the one here, had been fitted with top deck covers. Most of these covers were manufactured by Dick Kerr and Co. but in 1911 four were bought from Brush.

Right: Car no. 22 is parked at the original Bentley tram terminus and on the short spur off Bentley High Street. The Methodist Chapel in the background has since been demolished.

Below: Another view of car no. 24, this time on the passing loop near the junction of The Avenue and Arksey Lane.

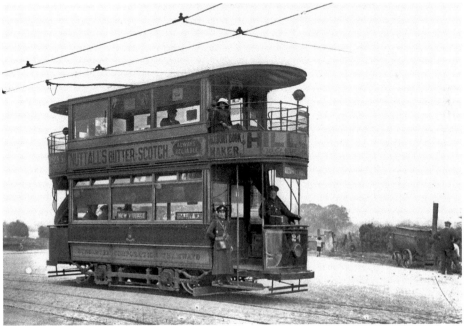

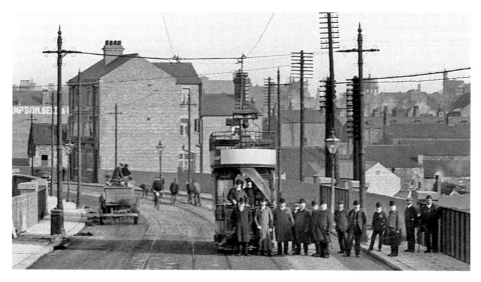

This is one of a set of photographs taken for Doncaster Corporation by local photographer Luke Bagshaw illustrating the progress of the North Bridge's construction. Fortunately, it is dated 2 May 1910 and depicts an official party posing for the camera before boarding the first tram across the New Bridge. Evidence suggests however that regular 'through' services to Bentley did not begin until a week later. A large scale civic opening of the bridge was postponed because of Edward VII's death and traffic used the New Bridge as soon as it was completed.

Prior to the opening of the New Bridge, the Bentley trams, when they needed major repairs, were towed by a steam roller over the Great Northern Railway Company's level crossing to the Grey Friars Road tram depot. This photograph was taken by Luke Bagshaw before the wiring for tram operations across the 'New Bridge' was completed; a Bentley tram is pictured adjacent.

Car no. 2 is passing over North Bridge on its way to the Racecourse. Initially on the opening of the New Bridge trams ran from Bentley through to the Racecourse, but this was not a success and was subsequently discontinued.

Originally when the Bentley trams travelled to the town centre, they terminated outside either the Guild Hall or the Electra Picture House in French Gate. Later, as the volume of traffic moving through the town began to increase, the terminus was moved to Trafford Street. Car no. 13, fitted with top deck cover and direct staircase passes the 'Brown Cow' public house, as it approaches the town centre.

Car no. 20 leaves North Bridge behind as it heads to the town centre loaded with passengers. The vehicle with fifty-six seats (34/22) was purchased in a batch of five, fleet nos 16-20 in 1903 from Dick Kerr and Co. Nos 18-20 had their lower saloons partitioned into smoking and non-smoking sections. No. 16 was withdrawn in 1930, nos 17-20 in 1927.

Car no. 13 working a cross-town service to the Racecourse; the Bridge Hotel is out of view to the right. St George's Church is in the distance on the left.

Car no. 3 on Arksey Lane makes its way to the Avenue. This vehicle was withdrawn in 1927 along with nos 1, 2, 4 and 5. All were sold to a Mr Buxton, (dealer and breaker) Tickhill Road, Doncaster. Most of these cars were broken up at Greyfriars Road Depot, but some were sold as garden sheds, and no. 3 still survived as such, at Green Lane, Scawthorpe, near Doncaster in 1973.

A Bentley tram leaves the outer terminus on the Avenue and heads to the town centre.

Car no. 14 at the Bentley New Village terminus, near the Avenue/Alexander Street junction. The 'Y' arrangement of track seen at many Doncaster tramway termini was abandoned on this later extension of the Bentley route in favour of a single line. The conductor is using a long bamboo pole to turn the trolley boom in preparation for the vehicle to make the return journey to Doncaster.

This is the Bentley town centre trolleybus terminus on North Bridge. The vehicles turned round at the terminus by utilising a 'turning circle' as demonstrated by the unidentified vehicle in the photograph. If, however, the vehicle was returning to the depot, a somewhat precarious procedure was followed. First of all, the trolleybus stopped on the bridge at a point immediately before the terminus; the trolleys were then unhooked and secured to clips on the roof. From there, the trolleybus then 'free-wheeled' for a short distance down the bridge and, when there was a convenient gap in the busy traffic, crossed over the road towards the Brown Cow public house. The trolleys were reattached here to enable the vehicle to return to the depot following the same route as it had used to begin services.

The Bentley route was the first to be converted by the specialists in overhead wiring, Messrs Clough & Smith, on 21 August 1928. It was a relatively easy job of double wiring with some single poles and brackets on Bentley Road and one bridge to pass under near the Don Bridge. Initial reaction to the trolleybuses on the Bentley route came in the form of complaints about radio interference from wireless 'hams'. Eventually after many experiments, condenser units and suppressors were fitted to the vehicles and this provided an effective measure to solve the problem. Garrett three-axled D/D trolleybus no. 4 with a Roe H32/28R body and BTH electrical gear and 60 hp motor is at the Bentley town centre terminus on North Bridge.

A trolleybus journey to and from Bentley took around 30 minutes. Usually five trolleybuses operated on this route, with six on Saturdays. Garrett trolleybus no. 3 approaches the stop outside St Peter's Church. The vehicle belongs to a batch of four acquired in 1928, fleet nos 1-4, registered nos DT 821-4, and was in service from 21 August 1928 to 30 April 1935. Nos 2-4 went to a Mr Buxton in May 1935 for scrap.

Trolleybus no. 4 again, this time outside the Grey Friars Road depot. Inspectors patrolled the routes regularly and woe betide anyone who was not doing their job properly. Waybills were left in a waybill holder on the platform and at busy periods an inspector could be round the bus before staff knew it. The no. 1 Bentley route was extended into a circular run round Bentley New Village.

Trolleybus no. 379 passes the Toby Jug public house under construction on 30 January 1955. On trolley routes, stops were marked by painting a white band round the green traction pole and stencilling Bus Stop on that in black letters. Therefore the stops were where the poles were, not necessarily at the most convenient places.

Trolleybus no. 381 in Bentley on 19 September 1955. The vehicle belongs to a batch of six 1949 BUT D/D trolleybuses, fleet nos 378-381, ex Darlington Corporation nos 68-73 with East Lancs. H30/26R bodies, English electrical gear and 120 hp motors. Nos 378-383 were all painted red with white window frames when first in service with DCT. All received the one white band livery during 1956-7 and all had emergency traction batteries until 1956. No. 381 was in service from 21 May 1952 until 12 November 1959 when it was withdrawn after an accident. Each vehicle was sold to Bradford City transport in January 1960, no. 378 was broken up for spares, nos 379-383 were rebodied with front entrance East Lancs bodies, becoming Bradford nos 831-835. All were withdrawn by Bradford during 1971.

1945 Sunbeam 'W' D/D trolleybus no. 386 is at speed crossing North Bridge on 31 December 1955. The vehicle is pictured with its Park Royal utility H30/26R body which was replaced between 28 November 1958 and 1 May 1959 with a Roe H34/28R replacement. The vehicle's lifespan was from 27 March to 1954 until 28 November 1961. The Roe body was subsequently fitted to a Daimler motorbus chassis fleet no. 168.

On leaving the Grey Friars Road depot, and before commencing services near the Brown Cow public house on North Bridge, the Bentley trolleybuses travelled via French gate, St Sepulchre gate, Station Road and Trafford Street. Trolleybus no. 382, in Trafford Street, was bought, together with five other trolleybuses, from Darlington Corporation in 1952. Following withdrawal in December 1959 all the vehicles were purchased by Bradford City Transport.

Karrier 'E6' D/D trolleybus no. 358 passes Bentley Pavilion (out of view on the left) on 3 Decmber 1955. After being in service from 1 May 1939, the vehicle had less than a month left in service when the picture was taken, being withdrawn on 31 December 1955. Nos 357-363 and 365 were disposed of to W. North (dealer) Leeds, (later Sherburn), February 1956. All were resold to Bolland (breaker), Wakefield, later in 1956 and broken up.

The Bentley trolleybuses did not terminate near the Bentley Colliery Workingmen's Club & Institute as the trams had done previously. Instead they continued along The Avenue, turned left along Victoria Road and back to Playfairs Corner via Askern Road. It was discovered however that most passengers used the service between the town centre and Playfairs Corner. Therefore any 'Special' trolleybuses operating on the Bentley route on Saturdays or at busy times during the week relieved those travelling on the 'normal' route by terminating and turning round at Playfairs Corner. No. 358, working on a Playfairs 'Special', after turning into Arksey Lane, is reversing along a short length of wire to rejoin the main route on 8 July 1955.

Trolleybus passing the Bridge Hotel on 6 February 1955. Note on the left the Toby Jug under construction and the George & Dragon Hotel on the right shortly before demolition. The mileage covered on the Bentley route was 2.70. The Toby Jug and Bridge Hotel have since been demolished.

Karrier 'E6' D/D trolleybus no. 360 leaves Bentley behind whilst travelling over the flood arches on its way to the town centre on 19 September 1955. At this point the vehicle had only until 18 November 1955 before being withdrawn.

No. 378, an ex Darlington Corporation trolleybus, passes the BRS Depot on North Bridge on 31 December 1955. Following the withdrawal on 25 February 1959 this vehicle was sold to Bradford City Transport in January 1960 and subsequently broken up for spares.

FIVE

Brodsworth Route

The *Doncaster Chronicle* of 18 September 1914 reported: 'A good start appears to have been made with the construction of the much needed tramway lines to the Woodlands Model Village. This very welcome extension of the Doncaster tramways is making excellent progress, as can be seen by anyone travelling between the town and the village. Just beyond the Great Central Avoiding line rails are already being placed in position. Further along the road, towards Highfields, a long trench has been dug for the purpose of making the concrete bed in which to lay the rails. Still further on sets of rails may be seen lying on the left-hand side of the road, and a long line of curb stones is seen on the opposite side of the road ready for use. A large number of men are engaged, and the construction of the tramway is finding very welcome employment at a time when work is none too plentiful.'

On leaving the Grey Friars Road depot, the Brodsworth trams travelled to French Gate where the crew, before beginning the journey to Brodsworth, turned the trolley round and altered the track points. Car no. 34, pictured in French Gate with the Royal Lancer pub to the right, was a sixty-six seater (40/26) and purchased in a batch of four, fleet nos 33-36, from Dick Kerr and Co. in 1916. These were unvestibuled, direct stairs, balcony cars mounted on Peckham 8 foot 6 inch P22 trucks. Nos 33 and 35 were withdrawn on 31 May 1932; nos 34 and 36 on 1 October 1933.

Tram operations began on the Brodsworth route during February 1916 and ceased on 8 June 1935. The route running along the west side of the Great North Road was double tracked as far as the Mill Bridge, with single track (and passing loops beyond). Although the Bentley and Brodsworth trams began the day's services in French Gate they did not return there on the inward journey as too much inconvenience was caused to other traffic passing through the town centre. Alternatively, they travelled into Trafford Street and commenced the remainder of the day's services from that point. Car no. 42, a sixty-six seater (40/26), is at the Trafford Street terminus with the Black Boy public house in the distance in French Gate.

There were several delays before the opening of the Brodsworth route. One of the reasons for this was Doncaster Corporation's dithering over whether to run trolleybuses or trams along the intended route. In the event the Adwick Urban District Council (the Woodlands' residents controlling body) in an effort to provide some form of transport for the area, threatened to license motorbus services. The dispute was resolved when both parties agreed to adopt a tramway system. Car no. 44, on York Road, belongs to the last group of cars acquired by the Corporation in 1920.

Right: Tramway staff posing somewhere along the Brodsworth tram route which was the only route not converted to trolleybus operations, becoming the Woodlands motorbus route. The Brodsworth route stretched for four miles, with eleven passing places on a single line.

Below: For several hours on Thursday, 21 October 1920, the tramway service between Doncaster and Brodsworth was interrupted after a collision between a Doncaster Corporation tramcar and a powerful traction engine. The consequences of the crash might have been much more serious as there were a fair number of passengers travelling on the tram, but apart from being shaken no-one was injured. The tractor, belonging to Messrs Edwards and Co. of Doncaster, was travelling from Doncaster with a couple of wagons. It met the tram about midway between the railway bridge, near the Sprotbrough Road turning and the Sun Inn, at a point where the road was narrow.

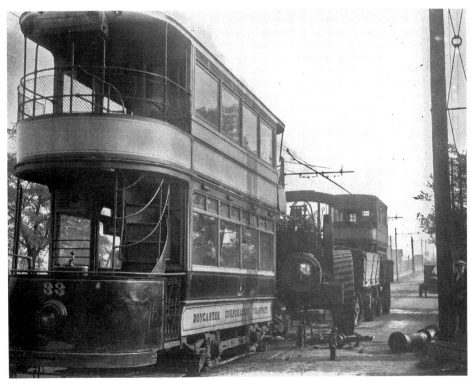

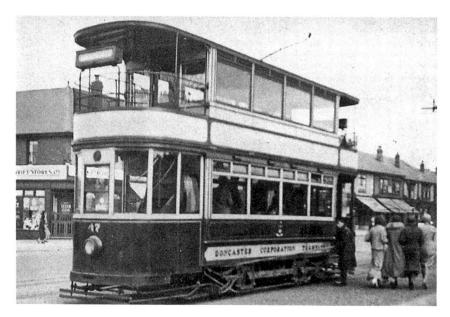

The Brodsworth route was so called because it was mainly intended to serve Brodsworth Colliery. But the route terminated in Woodlands and passengers travelling to the colliery had to walk the remainder of the way. The tram terminus was adjacent to the main road and opposite Windmill Balk Lane. Car no. 47 is at the Brodsworth terminus and one of the crew is preparing to change the trolley. The last Doncaster tram car ran on the Brodsworth route in June 1935, leaving a deficit of £168, 000 which was to be recouped by the new trolleybuses.

Towards the end of tram operations on the Brodsworth route the track had fallen into disrepair. At some points the trams could not even utilise the 'passing loops.' To help alleviate this problem the tram crews were issued with 'jumping irons'. These were short strips of metal that were placed on the track by either the conductor or driver to ensure that the tram's wheels were guided in the right direction when travelling over or using a 'passing loop.' Car no. 30 belongs to the batch of six, fifty-six seater (34/22), vehicles that were delivered in 1913. Although they were similar to previously acquired vehicles they arrived already fitted with top deck covers. For some time, these six cars were used almost exclusively on the Balby route.

SIX

Greyfriars Road

Here is car no. 1 shortly after delivery at the entrance to the Greyfriars Road tram depot. The man on the right of the photograph is probably Mr Wyld, the tramways' manager from 1902-4. Cars 1-25, bought in three batches in 1902-3, had 'open top' and 'ends', which at the time were almost universal tram features. Various firms, including Cravens of Sheffield, had submitted tenders to build Doncaster's trams, but the contract went to Dick Kerr and Co. of Preston, who later on supplied the entire fleet, except number 37 bought second hand from Erith in 1916. Refinements in the Dick Kerr trams included curtains, lengths of carpet on the lower deck seats – neither of which probably lasted long – and flap-over covers to keep the top deck seats dry whilst it was raining.

The electricity station (on the left) in Greyfriars' Road supplied power to the street lights of Doncaster from the end of 1899. The first supply of electricity to the general public was switched on by the Mayoress, Mrs Bentley at mid-day on 2 April 1900. The Corporation's charge for electricity in 1901 was 5*d* (2½p) per unit but following the commencement of the tramway service the extra demand for electricity was so high that the Corporation was able to spread the overhead charges and reduce the price per unit to 3*d* (1½p). The electricity works however made a loss of £4,625 in 1902, though a short time afterwards the tramways purchased half the station's output over a number of years, which helped the electricity department to become a leading source of energy in the town.

The Greyfriars Road electricity station continued to operate until the late 1950s when it was replaced by a new station at Crimpsall Ings.

The interior of the electricity station in Greyfriars' Road.

The Doncaster Corporation Tramways Electric Car Shed in Greyfriars Road. On the 2 June 1902 the Mayor of Doncaster Thomas Windle formally opened the tram shed door with an eighteen carat gold key.

The interior of the Greyfriars Road Electric Car Shed in 1902 showing four of the fifteen cars that were purchased in that year. Originally there were five roads in the shed with pits on roads 1-4 and enough space to accommodate five cars on each road. In 1916 two more roads (6 & 7) were added, together with short pits at the bottom of the shed and a spur to the rear, also with a pit. Space in this part of the shed was also utilised for the operation of machinery. As the trams were gradually phased out the shed was converted between 1928 and 1931 for trolleybus operation. Furthermore a 'washer' was introduced in 1955 on number one road and a new exit was created from one & two roads. Finally after changing ownership several times since its former use, the shed was demolished during the early months of 1983.

Above and below: Two views of a decorated open-top tram taken near the Greyfriars Road Depot, the vehicle playing a part in the town's peace celebrations.

The water car and snow broom, mounted on a 6 foot Brill 21E truck was in service from 1903-1935. I did have the large glass plate negative for this picture which was 'blacked out' round the vehicle. Eager to discover what was concealed I removed the mask only to find a brick wall!

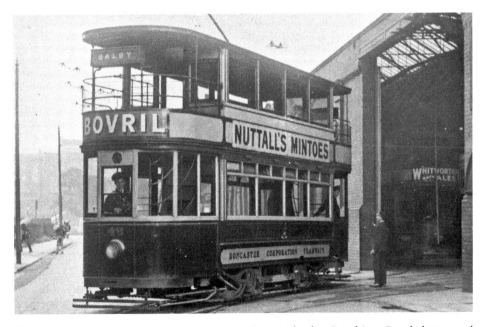

Dick Kerr sixty-six seat (40/26) car no. 46, is outside the Greyfriars Road depot, and belongs to the batch of trams fleet numbers 38-47 that was purchased in 1920. They were larger than most of the other vehicles, with four saloon windows and enclosed driver's platforms.

Dick Kerr trams, nos 38 and 46, are alongside trolleybuses nos 13 and 21 in the Greyfriars' Road depot.

Trolleybuses in the Greyfriars' Road depot on 9 April 1955.

SEVEN

Hexthorpe Route

Car no. 4 is working on the Avenue Road-Hexthorpe cross-town service. The Hexthorpe tram service itself was mainly used by workers from the Plant Works, Co-operative Stores, Burnett's Wagon Works and Woodhouse's Brass Works, with many fewer passengers at other times of the day. The total length of the Doncaster tram system was some nine miles and cost approx £77,500.

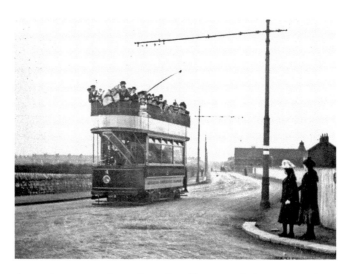

The suburbs of Hexthorpe, Hyde Park and Balby provided accommodation for many railway workers, and there was an acknowledged need for a public transport service to link these and other areas to the town centre. Car no. 4 is seen again here working on the first day of tram operations on the Hexthorpe route. It was noted that on Monday 2 June 1902 at the opening of the tramways the whole town was in jovial mood. The Chairman of the Electrical Committee, Councillor Dawson, presented Tramways Chairman Councillor Smith with a gold model controller handle in the form of a watch pendant, while Mr Beaton for the suppliers of the rolling stock, Messrs Dick Kerr, presented the Mayoress and Mrs Smith with miniature silver plated and ebony control handles.

With simple tools and equipment, labourers working for 5d (2½p) to 5½d (3p) an hour, lower a 'centre grooved' rail into position to establish a 'passing loop' at the corner of Spansyke Street in Hexthorpe. Although Doncaster and Hull were the only tramway systems to employ 'centre grooved' rails in the electric era, the Liverpool horse tramways and Dudley-Wolverhampton steam tramways had utilised a similar type of rail in the 1880s and 1890s. Besides travelling to work in the various factories in Hexthorpe people used the tram service to visit Hexthorpe Flatts, a popular recreation area, and only a short distance from the Bramworth Road terminus.

Car no. 14 at the Hexthorpe outer terminus in Bramworth Road. The first day's tram operations gathered £43 19s 5d for around 10,553 passengers carried, who paid, though hundreds more hitched free rides, overwhelming the conductors. The day after £34 3s was taken, though things were calmer by Wednesday morning when each car carried an average of twenty passengers.

Posing at the terminus in Bramworth Road with car no. 15 prior to the vehicle being fitted with a top deck cover, and direct staircase by Dick Kerr in 1913. Doncaster tram cars' livery was described as Midland Railway red and cream with gilt lettering and numerals.

Car no. 19 at Hexthorpe outer terminus, belongs to the 1903 batch of five vehicles purchased from Dick Kerr and Co., and was one of three vehicles with the lower saloons portioned into smoking and non-smoking sections.

Car no. 19, seen here again, passing through Hexthorpe. There were only two passing loops on the route and one of them may be seen here in the foreground. Before services had commenced in 1902 the route had been inspected by Lt Col. Major Druitt and Mr Trotter.

Car no. 16 passing the St Sepulchre Gate/West Street junction on its return journey to the town centre. The 'open' top deck of a tram was certainly pleasant to travel on during fine weather but when it was wet or cold passengers perhaps predictably tended to make for the lower deck. The Board of trade stipulated that trams could only carry eight standing passengers, consquently the passenger load was considerably reduced during bad weather and was obviously the reason for most cars to be fitted with 'top-deck covers' by 1913.

The YMCA building in St Sepulchre Gate stood at the junction of the Hexthorpe and Balby tram routes. Both the 'overhead' and 'track' points were always set for the Balby tram, which continued along St Sepulchre Gate into Balby Road. The 'Hexthorpe' crew had to alter these points to allow their trams to turn right and continue along the remainder of the route to the terminus in Bramworth Road. The latter line was single track, with 'passing loops' at the Plant Hotel and at Shirley Road. Car no. 13 was at the town centre terminus in Station Road prior to beginning its outward journey.

An unidentified tram working on the Hexthorpe route is pictured in Station Road with the Glyn Hotel as a back drop.

A view looking towards Printing Office Street finds car no. 28, purchased in 1913, parked in Station Road with the conductor adjusting the trolley boom for the vehicle to begin a trip to Hexthorpe. The tram on the left and in the background may be working on the Warmsworth route because by the time this picture was taken probably during the 1920s cars working on that route tended to terminate outside stationers Taylor & Colbridge's St Sepulchre Gate building instead of in Station Road.

The Urban Road/ Bramworth Road junction where car no. 19 is in a battered condition during the First World War while its female crew pose proudly for the camera along with the children on the top deck. Women were not employed on Doncaster's tramways until the outbreak of the War, replacing men who had responded to the call to arms. Initially, four conductresses began work in July 1915 and by the following Spring each one was a qualified tram driver. Also, at the outset nobody knew whether to call them 'motoress,' 'motorwoman,' or just simply 'driver'. As time passed most Doncaster trams were operated by women who were doing their bit for the War effort.

Car no. 29, a Dick Kerr fifty-six seater (34/22), glides along the route.

The Hexthorpe route was converted to trolleybus operation in July 1929, a short run with initially a ½d fare to a turning circle opposite the Dell. Karrier 'E6' D/D trolleybus no. 18 is working near the outer terminus on what appears to be a busy day. The vehicle was purchased in a batch of seven, fleet nos 17-23, in 1930 and in service from January 1930 until 31 July 1938. The Hexthorpe trolleybus route was service no. 3 and was threatened with closure in October 1953, being finally closed on 17 March 1962.

Karrier 'E6' D/D trolleybus no. 14, purchased in a group of six vehicles in 1929, is passing Morris's wallpaper warehouse and Scarborough Bros' 'four-gabled' edifice in St Sepulchre Gate West, whilst returning to the town centre. The livery of these early Doncaster trolleybuses was a kind of magnolia relieved by two maroon bands, the broader one around the waistline running to the cab area whose sides and front were totally maroon.

1945 Sunbeam 'W' D/D trolleybus no. 388 travels along French Gate passing Jackson's garage on the right whilst displaying the Hexthorpe route sign.

The Hexthorpe and Balby routes both had their town centre terminus in West Laith gate. From west Laith Gate, both the Hexthorpe and Balby trolleybuses joined St Sepulchre Gate, the main western road out of the town centre, via West Street. At the YMCA building the overhead points were set for the Balby trolleys to continue along St Sepulchre Gate into Balby Road. Therefore the Hexthorpe conductor, as in tram days, had to 'pull a switch' to change the overhead points before the vehicle could follow its correct route. In later years however, these points were changed automatically by the Hexthorpe driver 'drawing power' under a magnetic switch just before the junction. Ex Southend-on-Sea Sunbeam 'W' D/D trolleybus, fleet no. 384 is seen in West Laith Gate, 8 January 1955.

Karrier/Sunbeam 'W' D/D trolleybus no. 374 passes Bridge Terrace on its way into Hexthorpe. The vehicle was in service from 2 May 1945 until 15 October 1963, with a short spell out for rebodying between 31 October 1954 and 18 February 1955. C. W. Hatfield in his *Historical Notices of Doncaster* reveals that 'Bridge Street and Bridge Terrace were erected in 1853-54'. But the Plans Register in Doncaster Archives reveals that a number of the Bridge Terrace houses were not built until around 1880.

Rebodied 1947 Sunbeam 'W' D/D trolleybus no. 353 (with a 1958 Roe H34/28R body) passes the Scarll Road/Urban Road junction on its way to the Hexthorpe outer terminus. This was one of two vehicles, fleet nos 353-354, whose chassis were purchased second hand by DCT from the Mexborough & Swinton Traction Co. (nos 14 and 18) in 1958. The S/D Brush B39C bodies were removed by them. These were the last trolleybuses purchased by DCT. After withdrawal on 28 March 1963, the chassis of 353 went to Bolland (breaker), Wakefield, April 1963. The body fitted by Roe's went to a reconditioned 1951 Leyland PD2/1 chassis ex DCT 124.

Trolleybus using turning circle at the Hexthorpe outer terminus.

The trolleybus crews had to adhere to a strict time schedule on the Hexthorpe route. The outward and return journeys were only supposed to take 10 minutes each and there were a number of stops to make. Karrier/Sunbeam 'W' D/D trolleybus no. 374 is pictured with both the conductor and driver at the Hexthorpe terminus on 7 August 1954.

Trolleybus on Urban Road, Hexthorpe, while on its way to the outer terminus on 9 April 1955. The mileage covered on the Hexthopre route was 1.22.

Another view of Karrier/Sunbeam 'W' D/D trolleybus no. 374, just before crossing St James' Bridge, whilst on its way back to the town centre. To return to the depot at the end of the day's services, both the Balby and Hexthorpe trolleybuses changed trolleys at Jacob's Corner on to the Racecourse wires, ran along St Sepulchre Gate to Clock Corner, turned left utilising another set of wires and then travelled down French Gate to Greyfriars Road. Trolleybuses returning to the depot from other routes followed a similar course until in later years the vehicles travelled along Baxter Gate, changed wires near the Market place and reached Greyfriars Road via High Fishergate.

1945 Sunbeam 'W' D/D trolleybus no. 387 travels along a section of the Hexthorpe route which has seen much change since the picture was taken on 17 March 1962, with demolition and road widening taking place. There were two public houses almost facing each other, the Prior Well Inn seen on the right and the Hexthorpe House, out of view on the left, but both have since closed and been swept away.

Vehicles involved in dismantling the overhead trolley wires on the Hexthorpe route, 21 March 1962. Trolleybuses running costs were latterly £8,000 to £11,000 per week.

Left: Cutting the overhead wires on the Hexthorpe trolleybus system 21 March 1962.

Below: The first 'one-man' bus, operating on the Hexthorpe route, whilst the old overhead wiring system is being dismantled, 21 March 1962.

EIGHT
Hyde Park Route

The Hyde Park tram termini were situated in Station Road (Doncaster) and Jarratt Street (Hyde Park) though the latter was moved to Chequer Road in October 1902. Having left Station Road and when travelling along St Sepulchre Gate, the tram crew had to alter both an overhead point and a track point to enable the vehicle to turn left, continuing along Spring Gardens, Catherine Street and Carr House Road. The route was single tracked with a 'passing loop' in Catherine Street.

Dick Kerr car no. 14 pauses in St Sepulchre Gate East whilst displaying the Hyde Park route indicator. The picture is pre-1913 when the vehicle was fitted with a top deck cover and direct staircase, becoming a balcony car.

Behind the Hyde Park tram depicted here at the outer terminus near Chequer Road is an electric lamp used to illuminate the area. The Hyde Park route was only intended to stretch as far a Jarratt Street but with the construction of new streets along the route, the line was extended to Chequer Road. On the car's upper deck railings are brackets fitted in 1911 for a short-lived route letter system. The crew are wearing a uniform with peaked caps, possibly introduced about 1914. After the War plans were proposed to extend the Hyde Park route to the Racecourse and serve the new housing estates that were being planned on either side of Carr House Road. Yet, this was not undertaken until the route was converted to trolleybus operation in 1930. Motorman Horace Briggs together with a conductor and an inspector are with car no. 2.

Car no. 12 threads its way along Carr House Road whilst on a return journey to the town centre. Railway workers living in the rows of terraced houses along the Hyde Park route relied heavily on the tram services to take them to and from work. The houses on the right have since been demolished to make way for the town's Southern Relief Road.

The driver and conductress (just visible at the rear) with car no. 19 at the Hyde Park outer terminus. The tram, a 56 seater, was acquired in 1903 with its lower saloon partioned into smoking and non smoking sections, being withdrawn in 1927.

After leaving the Greyfriars depot, the Hyde Park trolleybus changed wires in St Sepulchre Gate from the 'depot' wires to the 'Racecourse' ones. After continuing a short distance and moving into the centre of the road, the bus changed trolleys again on to the 'Hyde Park' wires before commencing services in front of the Co-operative Emporium. Each 'circular' journey on the Hyde Park route took 20 minutes; normally two buses operated on the service. Karrier 'E6' D/D trolleybus no. 357 is at the town centre Hyde Park terminus on 12 March 1955, nine months away from being withdrawn on 31 December 1955, after sixteen years of service.

1945 Sunbeam 'W' D/D trolleybus no. 386 leaves St Sepulchre Gate West and enters Spring Gardens, making an outward journey on the Hyde Park route. The vehicle arrived in Doncaster during 1954 with a Park Royal utility H30/26R body, which was removed between 28 November 1958 and 1 May 1959 and replaced with a H34/28R fitted by Roe's.

Arriving in Doncaster in 1958, with a chassis from a Mexborough & Swinton Traction Co. S/D vehicle and then fitted with a 1958 Roe H34/28R body, trolleybus no. 354 is parked in Spring Gardens on Whit Saturday 9 June 1962.

Spring Gardens at the junction of Cleveland Street on the Hyde Park route, showing one of the problems of trolleybus operation – the need to wait until obstacles are removed. The leading trolleybus is no. 395 (EWT 480) an ex-Mexborough & Swinton Sunbeam vehicle. The Spring Gardens Methodist Chapel on the left has since been demolished.

At approximately 11.15 p.m. on 25 April 1958, trolleybus no. 385 collided with a single deck coach at the junction of Cleveland Street and Spring Gardens. No. 385 was the first Doncaster Corporation vehicle to be overturned. Fortunately there were no serious casualties. This vehicle was also originally withdrawn on 31 December 1961, but was reinstated on 1 February 1962 after a shortage of trolleybuses was caused by no. 371 being scrapped after an incident. No. 385 was temporarily withdrawn, the chassis overhauled, and then rebodied H34/28R by Roe's between 25 April 1958 and 1 December 1958. The vehicle was finally withdrawn on 5 September 1962.

Saturday work for the Hyde Park trolleybus crews is remembered for its tiring shift from 9.00 a.m to 11.20 p.m, thirty-five 'circular' journeys being made in this time. Rebodied 1943 Sunbeam 'D' D/D trolleybus no. 396, pictured in Spring Gardens near where the Southern Bus Station formerly stood, was purchased from the Mexborough & Swinton Traction Company in 1955 when surplus to requirements.

Leaving Spring Gardens behind rebodied 1943 Sunbeam 'D' D/D trolleybus no. 396. is crossing over St James' Street and turning into Catherine Street.

Rebodied 1947 Sunbeam 'W' D/D trolleybus no. 354 in Catherine Street on Whit Saturday 9 June 1962. The street was completely cleared in subsequent years.

A trolley approaches a waiting passenger at the Catherine Street/Carr House Road junction. All the buildings seen have since been cleared.

1945 Sunbeam 'W' D/D trolleybus no. 386 in Carr House Road on the last day of service on the Hyde Park route, 28 November 1961.

1945 Sunbeam 'W' D/D trolleybus no. 387 in Carr House Road on 5 December 1961.

Rebodied 1943 Sunbeam 'W' D/D trolleybus no. 395 pauses in Carr House Road on 21 November 1961. From this time the vehicle had another twelve months left in service, being withdrawn on 31 December 1962. Its chassis was purchased along with a Brush utility B35C body second hand from the Mexborough and Swinton Traction Co. in 1955. After withdrawal the body was fitted by Roes's to a new Leyland PD2/40 motorbus chassis, fleet no. 188. The properties on the right were demolished in later years for the construction of the Southern Relief Road.

The Hyde Park trolleybuses did not end the day's services at the terminus outside the Co-operative Society Emporium as the vehicle then faced the wrong direction to return to the depot. To solve the problem, the vehicles were changed on to the Wheatley Hills and Beckett Road wires at the Hall gate/Cleveland Street junction to enable the vehicles to reach Greyfriars Road via Cleveland Street, Printing office Street, St Sepulchre Gate and French Gate. The Hyde Park trolleybus route, service no. 6 was closed on 10 December 1961. Karrier 'E6' D/D trolleybus no. 363 is in Hall Gate on 25 September 1955. The vehicle was in service between 1 July 1939 and 27 January 1956.

After its accident trolleybus no. 385 was withdrawn from service until 1 December. During this time the vehicle was repaired and rebodied. The vehicle is seen on its return to services, travelling to the town centre via Catherine Street.

A trolleybus inches its way past a tower wagon at the Gill Street/Catherine Street junction while heading towards the town centre.

Karrier 'E6' D/D trolleybus no. 362 in Carr House Road on 2 April 1955.

Trolleybus turning into Spring Gardens after crossing the St James Street junction near the St James Street Baths. Demolition has taken place on each side of this southern end of Spring Gardens, ready for redevelopment.

Karrier/Sunbeam 'W' D/D trolleybus no. 372 waits to leave the north end of Spring Gardens at the junction with St Sepulchre Gate before completing the short run to the town centre on 11 November 1961. This vehicle, one of a batch of three, registered nos CDT 624 – CDT 626, acquired in 1945, saw service between 2 May 1945 until 15 October 1963 with a short interval between 5 July 1954 – 24 January 1955 for rebodying by Roe's.

NINE

Oxford Street Route

Driver Jack Haggitt and his conductor with their vehicle at the Oxford Street 'outer' terminus.

Doncaster Corporation, in planning its tramway routes, did not include any proposals for a service to Oxford Street. This decision was altered however when a petition was presented to the Corporation by the inhabitants of the West Ward requesting the introduction of a tram service. The route ran from Station Road along St Sepulchre Gate west to a junction at the YMCA building. From there it continued down Camden street, across St James Street to the top of Oxford Street and then along Upper Oxford Street to the terminus at Green Dyke Lane. Unfortunately the service did not prove to be a successful financial venture and was closed in April 1905. This photograph was taken looking down Camden Street towards St James' Schools on St Sepulchre Gate. It depicts passengers who are attending the Co-operative Society's gala on Burnett's field at Hexthorpe; they are boarding 'open top' and 'covered top' trams.

The folly of establishing a tramway route to Oxford Street was revealed in a record of the Tramway Department's receipts from the route, published in the *Doncaster Gazette* of 13 January 1905. Over a period of twenty-eight days £1 0s 8d was taken with only 248 passengers utilising the service. The scene above is at the Oxford Street/Green Dyke Lane junction.

TEN

Racecourse Route

Clock Corner was at the junction of the Avenue Road, Beckett Road and Racecourse routes. Trams also turned left here, along French Gate, when returning to the depot. The overhead points were always set for both the Avenue Road and Beckett Road trams, allowing them to continue from St Sepulchre Gate into Baxter Gate. To enable the Racecourse tram to follow the correct route, the conductor left his vehicle and changed the points by 'pulling a switch' suspended from a pole on the left hand side of the road; track points were also altered. When the car had successfully travelled from St Sepulchre Gate into the High Street it automatically re-set the overhead points and the conductor, having also re-set the track points, then rejoined the tram.

Car no. 1 makes its way through the bustling street life in the High Street, gathering speed on its way to the Racecourse.

Car no. 1 crawls patiently behind a fancy dress parade in Hall Gate during 1907.

Car no. 2 passes the Doncaster Mansion House on the left. Writing about the Racecourse route local tram enthusiast M. C. P. S. Bacon set the scene by stating: 'The Racecourse route of Doncaster Corporation tramways was more than ordinary interest in that it was a route laid down to meet a special set of conditions which occurred on certain days each year when race meetings were held on the Town Moor.' It was during the lifetime of tramways that the attendances at meetings reached what will probably be an all time peak, estimates of 500, 000 being usual, and when it is realised that the vast majority of these people arrived by train or stayed in the town for the period of the races it will be seen that the Tramways Department was faced with a very formidable task in conveying the crowds to and from the racecourse.

In High Street the Racecourse route had a uni-directional single line up to the Mansion House where there was a facing crossover from the inwards line, which turned into Priory Place. From there however the route was double track. Car no. 23 passes the elegant town houses in Hall gate whilst making its way to the Racecourse. This vehicle, a Dick Kerr fifty-six seater (34/22), was one of a batch of five, fleet nos 21-25, acquired in 1904. The picture is pre-1913 when the car was fitted with a top deck cover and direct staircase.

Car no. 1 at the top of Hall Gate on its outward journey. During the September race period in the first year of tram operations, all but two cars were used on the service to ferry race goers to the course.

Doncaster's centre-grooved rails are easily distinguishable here. So too are the lines of stone sets which were placed down each side of the rails. Most other tram systems had groves along the rail's inner edge. Car no. 8 is featured here at the junction of Hall Gate/South Parade.

Tram services to the Racecourse began at 7.00 a.m., each outward and return journey taking 10 minutes. Car no. 3 displaying the route letter R, passes Hall Cross Hill Bennetthorpe, in the days when it was a common sight to see a man walking a cow along the side of the road. This car had its lower saloon partitioned into 'smoking' and 'no smoking' sections and was one of only four cars that were not fitted with top deck covers. The sloping front (and back) of the car was to prevent passengers hitching a free lift on one of the bumpers.

M. Bacon (*op.cit.*) describes what it was like to leave the races and travel by tram on St Leger Day at the Racecourse: '... we come out of the course and make for the Grand Stand Terminus. Here we see forty or more cars slowly moving round the large turning circle collecting a full complement of passengers as they move. We make for one of the brand new ... cars, and being fortunate, manage to get a seat on the forward balcony. We have more time to look round and notice that the car has a crew of four, a driver, two conductors and last but not least a six-foot policeman whose duty it is to remove any non-paying passengers "using no more force than is necessary."'

By following a 'circular' track at the 'southern end' of Town Moor Avenue, trams were able to turn round at the Racecourse 'outer' terminus without the trolley being changed. On race days this eased the Tramway Department's formidable task of keeping a continuous flow of trams moving. The decorated car (car no. 21) is seen using the 'circular' track on Coronation Day, 1911. The building on the right was used as a police station during race meetings.

The Racecourse route was unprofitable except when catering for either a race or football crowd. In the week ending 11 December 1913 only 2,769 passengers used the service and takings were below £11.

The foreground here gives an indication of the complex track layout extending from Bennetthorpe to the Racecourse 'outer' terminus in Grandstand Road. Pointwork throughout the system was changed by the conductor using an iron for the rails and a stirrup on the post for the overhead.

M. Bacon makes two interesting observations about tram workings on Race days: 'First there were on each race day the Police cars. These were two open top cars which, about 10.00 a.m. pulled up in front of the Guidhall and which were each loaded with fifty six policemen and one inspector. This awe inspiring load was then conveyed down to the course and the sight of these cars, each with fifty six policemen, each with his helmet tilted at regulation angle was something I, for one, will never forget ... the second special working was the "bullion tram". This car, again usually an open top deck, driven by a member of the depot staff ran each morning from the Tramways' Office in Greyfriars Road along French Gate, over Clock Corner and along High Street to what was then Becketts Bank and it was loaded with the takings of the day before. In this way the money was transferred from the Tramways Office to the Bank.' Car no. 17 struggles with crowds as it attempts to leave the Racecourse; the view was probably taken from an upstairs room in Bell Vue House(now the Grand St Leger Hotel).

By 1927 car no. 19 was among the vehicles withdrawn and dismantled at the Greyfriars Road depot by a local scrap dealer. Some tram bodies were sold off as garden sheds, one at least went to Wath, and it is thought a number of 'trucks' saw further service at Hull.

Car no. 5 in South Parade approaches the junction with Hall gate on its return journey to the town. The vehicle passes what is now the Regent Hotel on the right and this was also in the days before there was a cinema at the Hall Gate/Thorne Road junction.

The Cuttriss family arrived in Doncaster during the late nineteenth century and before establishing a motorcar garage and subsequent model shop they ran a High Street dentist's practice. This view of a race-day crowd was taken from their balcony. The Ram Hotel, on the right, was later rebuilt as the Danum Hotel. On the corner of Cleveland Street/Hall gate is Mark Dowson's gentleman's outfitter's shop; Dowson was Tramway's chairman 1905-1908. In 1913 it was proposed to lay a tram line along Silver Street (out of view on the left) linking High Street with Sunny bar. The line was to be principally used by the Avenue Road and Beckett Road cars. The idea, however, did not materialise until the trolleybus era when the Wheatley Hills and Beckett Road trolleys travelled along Silver Street and Cleveland Street on their return to the town centre.

The single line extending from the Station Road terminus to the Mansion House caused acute congestion, when trams were operated for the first time during Race Week, September 1902. The build up of cars waiting to either leave or return to Station Road made it imperative that an alternative line via the terminus and High Street should be made. In the ensuing months work began on a line along Priory Place and Printing Office Street, thus making the necessary relief route between the two points. Car no. 5 is seen prior to following this route.

Karrier 'E6' D/D trolleybus no. 23 on a wet evening outside Hodgson & Hepworth's building along St Sepulchre Gate. No. 23 was supplied free to the Corporation by Karriers as a substitute for vehicle no. 22 which was used as a demonstration vehicle.

In the early stages of trolleybus operations on the Racecourse route the vehicles turned round at Belle Vue House (now grand St Leger Hotel). However, when Carr House Road was transformed during the 1930s into a main road it enabled both the Racecourse and Hyde Park routes to become 'circular' routes. The Racecourse route, service no. 6, ran from Bennetthorpe along Carr House Road and back to the town centre on the same course as the Hyde Park route. Also the clockwise service was labelled Racecourse and the anti-clockwise Hyde Park. The trolleybus here is in South Parade.

Although both the Hyde Park and Racecourse 'circular' trolleybus routes were capable of taking passengers to and from the Racecourse, trolleybuses were operated around the 'circle' in the Hyde Park direction only during Race Week. This method was considered to be the best way for trolleybuses to disperse the many thousands of people visiting the Racecourse each year. Two trolleys are passing in Bennetthorpe prior to house building along the thoroughfare.

Dick Kerr tram no. 7 and Garrett three-axled D/D trolleybus no. 1 pictured together on the Racecourse route with Belle Vue House on the left. Trolleybus no. 1, registered no. DT 821, saw service between 3 April 1928 and 31 July 1938. The cost of the first eight trolleybuses was £2,105 each.

Karrier 'E6' D/D trolleybus no. 22 is in Bennetthorpe and operating on a 'special' whilst heading towards the Racecourse. The vehicle had a Roe H32/28R body, BTH electrical gear and 60 hp motors. It saw service from December 1930 until 30 April 1945. In January 1930 it went to Johannesburg, South Africa, and also to York, England in December 1930 as a Karrier Demonstrator. In August 1945 it went to a Mr Buxton, Tickhill Road, Doncaster for scrap.

Karrier 'E6' D/D trolleybus no. 27 loads passengers adjacent to the Racecourse. The vehicle had a lifespan of eight years July 1931 to 30 June 1939.

On leaving the Greyfriars Road depot the Racecourse trolleybuses commenced services by travelling along French Gate and joining its route wires in High Street.

Garratt three-axled D/D trolleybus, fleet no. 1, is outside Eastfield House on Grandstand Road shortly after delivery to the Corporation in 1928. Between 3 April 1928 and 20 August 1928 and 1 June 1936 and 31 July 1938, this vehicle was used for training trolleybus drivers.

Karrier/Sunbeam 'W' D/D utility trolleybus no. 369 on Carr House Road. This vehicle was one of three fleet nos 69-71 (renumbered 369-371, 1947), purchased in 1943. No. 369 was out of service being rebodied H34/28R by Roe's between 31 May 1954 and 4 January 1955.

Karrier 'E6' D/D trolleybus no. 347 operating on a Racecourse Special, gathers speed on its return to the town centre. Note that a 6d standard fare is being charged. The vehicle saw service between 12 July 1938 and 30 October 1955.

Trolleybus operations on the Racecourse route survived a threat of abandonment in 1952, but were temporarily displaced by motorbuses from June to November 1954, owing to both the widening of the road and re-positioning of 'trolley' poles in Bennetthorpe. Karrier/Sunbeam 'W' D/D utility trolleybus no. 377 is outside Blakes' store in St Sepulchre Gate at the Racecourse town centre terminus on 8 January 1955.

Karrier/Sunbeam 'W' D/D utility trolleybus no. 375 in Carr House Road on 6 Oct 1963. In the mid-1950s staff shifts were about eight hours long, with a short break, with three journeys completed every hour. The fares were simple just 1d for a child and 1½d adult.

Karrier Bantam Tower Wagon registered no. EDT 21 is in Bennetthorpe and saw service from 1946 to 1964. Afterwards it went to a Mr Carpenter, Decoy Bank, Doncaster, for scrap.

An unidentified trolleybus speeds along Bennetthorpe past the Rockingham on its way to the Racecourse.

Karrier/Sunbeam 'W' D/D utility trolleybus no. 376 in Carr House Road. The mileage covered on the Racecourse route was 2.90.

Trolleybus no. 375 on Racecourse roundabout.

ELEVEN

Staff and Aftermath

Initially, thirty-five tram drivers and conductors were employed and they each worked fifty-four hours per week. A driver earned a maximum wage of £1 7s 0d (£1 3p) whilst a conductor received £1 2s 6d (£1 12½p). A standard fare of 1d was charged on all routes, special rates and reductions being introduced during Race Week. Red penny counters were introduced in 1911 and were sold to the public at fourteen for a shilling but were withdrawn after misuse; passengers sometimes supplemented their stock of counters with red buttons and presented them to the conductors during the darkest part of the day! The staff of car no. 13 pose at Hexthorpe.

Tram conductor and driver.

Tram conductor faces camera with
Red House, St Sepulchre in the
background.

A Tramways staff group which includes women. The first Electrical & Tramway Manager was Mr E. S. Rayner, while the Superintendent was Mr A. E. Blower. Early Inspectors were R. Cook and J. W. Saunders. Mr Tommy Potts was Transport Manager for much of DCT's existence.

The Tramway Department's maintenance staff.

Michael Fowler started as a student trolleybus conductor in December 1955 having the following to say about ticket machines at that time: 'For short and busy runs the Ultimate ticket machines were ideal. The five compartments accommodated 1d, 1½d, 2½d and 3d rolls of tickets, although the maximum fare on the trolleybuses at that time was 2½d!' After his first shift he stated: 'At 3 p.m. I retired exhausted at the end of my first shift [he'd started at 6.30 a.m.], even though I'd been "coupled up" with an experienced conductor, to discover the delights of "cashing in", again at the Station Road premises. The tough paper money bags and the stiff leather cash bag had torn the skin around my finger nails considerably, but at least I had made it without dropping too many clangers, and I could now make my journeys home free of charge as an employee, saving all of 1½d.'

A group of Tramways employees.

Karrier 'E6' D/D trolleybus no. 333 and Karrier 'E6' D/D trolleybus no. 332 after withdrawal. No. 32 was acquired in 1934, fleet no. 32, and renumbered 332 in 1947. The chassis was chrome plated for exhibition on the Karrier stand at the 1933 Commercial Motor Show at Olympia. In later years the vehicle ran almost exclusively on the Bentley route with a dent in the front offside. The body incorporated many details to Mr Potts' (Transport General Manager) own design. The motor was never removed during the whole of the vehicle's life, stretching between 1 January 1934 to 8 May 1952. Following withdrawal no. 32 went to Bell Bros (breakers), Decoy Bank, Doncaster, for scrap in 1953.

Three trolleybuses stored after withdrawal at Leicester Avenue, Intake, Doncaster.

Karrier/Sunbeam 'W' D/D utility trolleybus no. 371 and motorbus no. 60 are in Arnold's breaker's yard at Black Bank on 12 April 1962. No. 371 in service from 5 November 1943 until 29 January 1962 was withdrawn after an accident with a Felix Motors' bus.

After being in service from 7 March 1935 to 16 May 1952, Karrier 'E6' D/D trolleybus no. 334 went to Stainton Cricket Club as a pavilion during July 1952. It was sold for scrap by June 1963 and is pictured here on 14 April 1962.